D0989798

A MOTHER'S MEMORY JOURNAL

Look back · Record · Treasure forever

quadrille

THIS MOTHER'S MEMORY
JOURNAL IS A GIFT TO

_____

WITH LOVE FROM

_____

Given name at birth

Date of birth

Place of birth

Relationship / marriage

Children

YOUR YOUTH

Your grandparents' names

Your grandparents' dates of birth

Where were your grandparents born?

What were your grandparents' occupations?

What did you enjoy most about your grandparents' company?

What memories did your grandparents share with you from their childhood?

Have you inherited any precious keepsakes from your grandparents?

Do you, or I, resemble any of our ancestors?

Your mother's name

Your mother's date of birth

Your mother's place of birth

Your mother's occupation

Your father's name

Your father's date of birth

Your father's place of birth

Your father's occupation

How did your parents meet?

What's your earliest memory of your mother and father?

Did your parents have a happy marriage?

How strict were your parents?

What did you admire about your parents?

Who were the members of your immediate family?

Names of your siblings

Your first family home

Your family pets

Describe the first bedroom you can remember

Which family games did you love playing together?

What was your most precious toy?

Describe a garden or park you remember playing in

What frightened you as a child?

What can you remember about your first day at school?

How well did you do in your exams?

Which television programmes did you love to watch?

Did you take part in a school play or a sports team?

What was your favourite Christmas present?

What was the worst trouble you got into at school?

Where was the best holiday you enjoyed as a child?

What did you want to be when you grew up?

Who was your best friend?

What was life like as a teenager?

What did you argue with your mother about?

Can you recall one special day with your mother?

Where (or what) was your first job?

When did you learn to drive?

Did you have a favourite outfit?

When did you leave home?

Describe your first love

What piece of advice would you pass back to your 21-year-old self?

Where did you and father meet?

What first attracted you to him?

When (and how) did you know you had fallen in love?

How did you both make up after an argument?

Describe a special moment in your relationship

Share any secrets you've discovered about sustaining a happy relationship

STARTING A FAMILY

Names of your children

Dates of birth of your children

Where were they born?

Were there any children that are no longer here?

Did you plan to have a family?

What was my father's reaction when you announced the pregnancy?

How strong was your maternal instinct?

What most excited you about being pregnant?

Did you have any fears about your pregnancy?

What advice did your mother share about being pregnant?

How uncomfortable or happy were your nine months with me?

Did you read any birthing or baby manuals?

Tell me about the day I was born

How easy / dreadful were your labours?

What names did you decide not to call me?

What does my name mean?

What would you have called me if I were the opposite sex?

Describe the feeling when you were first left on your own with me as a baby?

Did the mother and baby bonding come easily?

As a new mother, how long did the period of sleepless nights continue?

How did my father help during the sleepless nights?

Did you have a particular way of getting me to sleep?

Did you connect with me through breast or bottle-feeding?

What was the worst accident I had as a baby or toddler?

Is there any advice you followed about raising a baby that you would not follow if you had your time again?

When was I weaned, and what was the first food you fed me?

Did you feel lonely as a new mother?

Did you ever doubt your capabilities as a mother?

Share one piece of advice for looking after newborns

A family tree is a diagram which charts the relationships of each generation within a family. The branches of the tree connect each person to their parents, spouses and children.

You can start with the oldest generation at the top and the newer generations at the bottom. You can make it more complete by adding branches for cousins, aunts and uncles, or keep it focused and create a family tree with only parents, grandparents and siblings – it can be as simple or as detailed as you like. For extra detail, you can record both maiden and married names, as well as dates of births and deaths.

FAM
TR

MILY

EE

BRINGING ME UP

What gave you confidence as a young mother?

Did you enjoy going to playgroups or mother-and-baby coffee mornings?

Which bedtime stories did we read together?

How did you potty train me?

Who did you spend most of your time with when I was young?

How did you carry me around – a papoose or a pram?

What did we see on our first trip to the cinema or theatre?

Were there any particular rules that you tried to make me follow?
Set bedtimes / table manners?

Did you ever lose me in a crowd?

What were your techniques for dealing with tantrums?

What was the naughtiest thing I ever did?

When did you feel the most exasperated?

What was the silliest thing I ever did?

Describe an ordinary meal we ate together after school

What was my first word?

What used to make us all fall about laughing?

Recall our first holiday as a young family

What craft activities did we enjoy doing together?

How did you manage when I was ill?

Which piece of music reminds you of those years?

Can you remember making or buying any special birthday cakes?

How did your growing family impact on your finances?

What was the first job you did after having children?

Were you happy about returning to work?

Who did you trust to look after me when you were away or working?

What was the hardest thing you've watched me go through?

Did I ever ask more of you than you were able to give?

Is there an object from my childhood that you still treasure?

Can you describe the love you felt for me as a child?

TEENAGE YEARS

Describe how your mothering changed as I entered my teenage years

What kept you awake at night when I was a teenager?

When was our relationship hardest?

What was our worst row about?

What did you think of my friends?

What did I want to be when I grew up?

Did you have to encourage me to do my homework?

How did you feel when I began my first relationship?

What was the most fun we had together?

Did you see your younger self in me?

What was your main hope for me as I grew into an adult?

What would you have done differently as a mother?

BEING A MOTHER,
BEING YOU

Did becoming a mother change your sense of self?

What similarities do you share with your mother?

What similarities do you share with me?

Has being a mother made you reflect on your relationship with your mother?

How did becoming a mother impact on your relationship with my father?

Do you have any regrets as a mother?

What do you think you got right as a mother?

What about motherhood has given you the most pleasure?

Are there any parenting mistakes you would not like me to repeat?

How do you measure success as a mother?

What would you like to be remembered for?

What has been the happiest time of your life?

What's the most moving book you've read?

If you were stranded on a desert island which one item would you take?

What compromises have you made to get where you are today?

When was the saddest time of your life?

Who or what has sustained you through troubling periods?

What do you like and dislike about modern life?

What would you like to bring back from your childhood?

What do you think has been the greatest invention in your lifetime?

How have you observed attitudes to women changing?

What has been the greatest social change for the better in your lifetime?

Describe a moment in history that you will never forget

FUTURE GENERATIONS

Record the most valuable piece of advice you have been given

Share a favourite family recipe

Are there any family health issues we should discuss?

Are there any family heirlooms that are particularly meaningful?

Is there an aspect of Christmas or other festivities that our family has always celebrated in a particular way?

Which family traditions would you like us to continue?

Record family quotes that have passed down the generations

Describe a famous family anecdote

What is your most precious wish for future generations of our family?

BUSINESS DEVELOPMENT DIRECTOR Melanie Gray

EDITOR Zena Alkayat

AUTHOR Joanna Gray

DESIGNER Katherine Keeble

PRODUCTION DIRECTOR Vincent Smith

PRODUCTION CONTROLLER Stephen Lang

Published in 2018 by Quadrille,
an imprint of Hardie Grant Publishing

Quadrille
52–54 Southwark Street
London SE1 1UN
quadrille.com

All rights reserved. No part of this publication may be
reproduced, stored in a retrieval system or transmitted
in any form by any means, electronic, mechanical,
photocopying, recording or otherwise, without the
prior written permission of the publishers and
copyright holders.

The moral rights of the author have been asserted.

Copyright text © Quadrille 2018
Copyright design © Quadrille 2018

ISBN 978 1 78713 263 4
Printed in China